Teaching Thinking Skills: Social Studies

Karen Rosenblum-Calé

Produced in cooperation with
the NEA Mastery In Learning Project

nea **PROFESSIONAL LIBRARY**
National Education Association
Washington, D.C.

Copyright © 1987
National Education Association of the United States

Note

The opinions expressed in this publication should not be construed as representing the policy or position of the National Education Association. Materials published as part of the Building Students' Thinking Skills series are intended to be discussion documents for teachers who are concerned with specialized interests of the profession.

Library of Congress Cataloging-in-Publication Data

Rosenblum-Calé, Karen.
  Teaching thinking skills.

  (Building students' thinking skills)
  "Produced in cooperation with the NEA Mastery in Learning Project."
  Bibliography: p.
  1. Thought and thinking—Study and teaching.
2. Social sciences—Study and teaching. 3. Cognition in children. I. Title. II. Series.
LB 1590.3.R67 1987   300'.7   86–18034
ISBN 0-8106-0680-1

CONTENTS

Introduction 5

Thinking 8

Teaching Thinking: A Review of the Literature 10

A Classroom Environment That Promotes Thinking 15

    The Environment 15
    The Methodology 18

Learning Social Science: The Curriculum, Grade by Grade 21

    The Primary School Experience 21
        Pre-operational Stage (to age 7) 24
        Operational Stage (ages 7 to 11) 24
    The Middle/Junior High School Years:
    Developmental Considerations 26
        Curriculum Focus:
        The Student as an Individual and a Citizen 28
        Integrating Thinking Skills into the Curriculum 32
    The High School Years:
    Developmental Considerations 36
        Social Studies as an Academic Discipline 36
        A Focus of Instruction:
        Ethical and Normative Issues 40

Conclusion 45

Bibliography 47

The Author

Karen Rosenblum-Calé is a Research Associate of the Institute for Interdisciplinary Studies, Santa Monica, California. She has taught at Holyoke College, University of Southern California, Lafayette College, and the University of Arizona.

The Advisory Panel

Jesus Garcia, Associate Professor, Department of Educational Curriculum and Instruction, College of Education, Texas A & M University, College Station

Ronald G. Helms, Executive Director, Ohio Association for U.S. History and Government Educators, Centerville

Peter Huybers, History teacher, Hillside Junior High School, Simi Valley, California

Shirley J. Johnson, Social Studies teacher, William Wirt Middle School, Riverdale, Maryland

James E. Krolikowski, Social Studies teacher, Manchester Memorial High School, New Hampshire

Thinking Skills Series Editors

Marcia Heiman is Director, Learning to Learn Program, Boston College, Chestnut Hill, Massachusetts. Joshua Slomianko is Co-Director, Learning Skills Consultants, Cambridge, Massachusetts.

INTRODUCTION

> Our nation is at risk. . . . If an unfriendly foreign power had attempted to impose on America the mediocre educational performance that exists today, we might well have allowed this to happen to ourselves. . . . We have, in effect, been committing an act of unthinking, unilateral educational disarmament. (19, p. 23)*

In 1983, the National Commission on Excellence in Education, in an essay intended to be "as much an open letter to the American people . . . as a report to the Secretary of Education" (19, p.24) opened what has become known as "the great school debate."

"Our society and educational institutions," the Commission continues, "seem to have lost sight of the basic purposes of schooling, and of the high expectations and disciplined effort necessary to attain them" (19, p. 24). The data cited were familiar: functional adult illiteracy, declining aptitude and achievement test scores, the proliferation of remedial needs and classes, and employees lacking in those basic skills necessary for satisfactory job performance. Moreover:

> Many 17 year olds do not possess the "higher-order" intellectual skills we should expect of them. Nearly 40% cannot draw inferences from written material; only one-fifth can write a persuasive essay; and only one-third can solve a mathematics problem requiring several steps. (19, p. 26)

In short, many of those who could read, write, and add could not think or reason.

In this great debate, it was easier for Americans to agree that a problem exists than to decide on its cause and remedy. To some, the source of the "dis-ease" lay in past decades of permissiveness; the cure was a return to basics, emphasizing skills in reading, writing, and mathematics, along with accompanying discipline and dress codes. Others looked toward the promise of high technology, encouraging the introduction of computers as learning aids in all schools and the training of students in their use. For still others, the key actor was the teacher; if teachers were better paid, or rewarded according to their performance, a better quality of educator would be attracted to the classroom.

These perspectives, often posed as opposites, in fact are not. Nor are they sufficient, if the objective of education is, in the words of psycholo-

---

*Numbers in parentheses appearing in the text refer to the Bibliography beginning on page 47.

gist Erich Fromm (10), to produce "better" and "more successful" human beings. Basic skills are tools or means for problem solving, but first the existence of a "problem" must be felt and comprehended. Technology can be a learning or management device, but first the machines must be invented and improved. Furthermore, few would opt for a strictly utilitarian world in which there is no place for individual taste and creativity.

From the standpoint of the community, education is a means of perpetuating social continuity; it transmits a society's standards, behavior patterns, and techniques to the young. From the perspective of the individual, it is a process that should make possible the realization of his or her human potential. In the interaction between individual and society, both must change; the society is affected by the actions of individuals, and the individual responds to society and assimilates its events. Education is dynamic and continuous; unlike formal schooling, it never stops. Therefore, the objective of formal schooling is to enable people to continue their education beyond the classroom; to provide them with skills and information that will help them understand and shape their futures.

Sometimes such formal instruction is directed mainly at the development of the intellect (4). Others stress the process of doing—not confining the concept to motor behavior, but embracing the active agent "at the center of his [her] own actions" who "plans, directs, controls and judges" (16, p. 5). Again, the differences are largely those of emphasis; the first group might focus on the development of reason as a guideline for action, while the second is more concerned with the whole personality. Both would agree that children are in the classroom to learn to use their minds, and not merely to absorb "lessons." The task of the teacher is then not only to impart knowledge, but also to encourage students to respond to their environment in an increasingly sophisticated way.

It is generally assumed that one of the tasks of the school is to teach children how to think. But what exactly is meant by *thinking*? Is it the same as learning? Is it synonymous with reasoning? If so, is there a place for the less rational phenomena of intuition, insight, and imagination? Does thought need to have an object—a problem to be solved? Or should the teacher also encourage random musing, speculation, contemplation? Must thought lead to knowledge or truth? Or outside of the hard sciences, should the aim be to develop the best possible argument? Should all subjects be thrown open for classroom scrutiny, including those that parents or community groups do not want to debate?

Apart from the subject matter, can thinking, as a process, be taught at all? To all students, or only to the "gifted"? What is the role of the teacher: initiator, facilitator, or judge? Is it possible for teachers, given all their other obligations and priorities, to devote sufficient time and energy to encourage students to "think for themselves" without sacrificing other goals and ends that they value and are required to attain?

Such questions have a particular urgency for teachers of the social sciences, a discipline that studies social, economic, and political activities, including the relationships between people and their environment, with each other, and with themselves. There are those who believe that such subjects *can* be objectively studied through value-free inquiry; that mainly data relating to finite objects or behavior should be used; and that conclusions should revolve around effects that can be readily confirmed. Others insist that no one can escape from the biases inherent in her or his own culture and that in avoiding the dilemma of making value judgments, the subject matter becomes too narrow to be meaningful.

Because social studies, particularly as it is taught in the public schools, includes civics, citizen education, instruction in democratic values, consumer education, and marriage and the family, the curriculum often conveys a definite message, which is already widely shared. Such a situation is inevitable when schools are also socializing agents. Furthermore, because the norms upheld include self-expression, a diversity of values, the tentativeness of propositions and conclusions, and the competition of ideas, students' involvement in critical and creative thinking may actually be encouraged.

Nonetheless, in particular environments, a gap can exist between the professed ideals and the latitude of debate that is actually welcomed. The degree of difficulty this poses for teachers who include critical thinking instruction in their classrooms will depend on their specific environment and the definition they accept of the thinking process and its goals. These are dilemmas not faced so directly by teachers of more "neutral" subjects—i.e., mathematics and the natural sciences.

THINKING

Thinking is a natural act. Ernest Dimnet's characterization of the thinker, that "the thinker is a man [or woman] who sees where others do not" (9, p. 33), is more a description of people's unused potential than of the limitation of their minds. Children, and adults who have never been to school, think every day.

The word *think*, as Alan R. White (28) points out, encompasses many aspects of the active intellect. Thinking can signify meditation or daydreaming; it can result from paying attention when performing a task or observing a scene. It can signify the ability, when confronted with a problem, to identify what the problem is about, to take steps in the search for an answer, or to come up with the "right" answer. Thinking can lead one to form an opinion, understand a concept, or have an insight.

The human being, as philosopher Blaise Pascal wrote long ago, is a "thinking reed" (20); he or she observes, classifies, compares, and concludes in order to make the universe intelligible. As an individual matures, she or he develops a "cognitive map," in which thought and emotion are intertwined. According to Milton Rokeach (23), this map forms a sort of screening system by which incoming stimuli are sorted.

To behaviorists, thoughts are set off in the process of problem solving. Cues in the outside world call forth intellectual strategies that have previously resulted in the reward of problem solution; as the learner varies these responses, feedback on the accuracy of the strategies shapes the learning process. Psychologist Jean Piaget has concluded that the ability to solve problems develops naturally as a child matures physically. Between birth and the age of seven—Piaget's pre-operational stage—a child is unable to carry out such mental operations as subsuming objects in a class, putting items in a series, or reversing processes. These tasks can be performed and symbols understood and used during the stage of concrete operations, between the ages of seven and eleven. Finally, between the ages of ten and fourteen, the stage of formal operations, an individual is able to reason and make deductions abut subjects unrelated to his or her direct experiences.

Many people have pointed out the "natural" curiosity of children; that "all children under nine or ten years of age are poets and philosophers" is one viewpoint (9, p. 38). Thereafter, children increasingly imitate their elders; as adults, they may be content to have the same thoughts, opinions, and behavior patterns as everybody else. The questions to be asked are these: How "creative" and "questioning" should a child be encouraged to be? And can thinking be taught in a classroom? Or should care mainly be taken not to damage or extinguish those mental processes—whether intuitive, exploratory, or rationally goal-directed—through which children already handle their nonacademic lives?

TEACHING THINKING: A REVIEW OF THE LITERATURE

Some educators regard thinking as a *process*, as a set of procedures or a series of identifiable skills that can be taught, either apart from or integrated with particular subject matter content. Others regard it broadly as an *experience* in which the student engages, alone or with peers, under the guidance of a teacher. The two perspectives are not discrete: in practicing a thinking skill, students are involved in the exercises they are working out; later in the course of an activity, they are led to identify the skills and procedures they have (perhaps unconsciously) used. Formal programs often integrate the two approaches, following the thinking skills exercises with participatory/role-playing experiences. The differences between these approaches correspond to those between the "intellect" and the "holistic doer/actor."

John Michaelis (18) identifies six types of thinking skills, the "lower" being perception, association, and concept attainment, and the "higher," problem solving, critical thinking, and creative thinking. By *perception*, he means "discriminating and differentiating"; by *association*, the recognition of relationships; and by *concept attainment*, the abstraction or generalization of properties (18, pp. 72-73). *Problem solving* involves the use and mastery of the following steps: recognizing and defining the problem, forming tentative solutions or hypotheses on the basis of experience, organizing and interpreting data, and drawing and verifying conclusions (18, p. 77). *Critical thinking* implies the making of "evaluations in terms of standards and criteria" (18, p. 78); *creative thinking* leads to the realization of something "new" or "original" (18, p. 80). Michaelis would integrate instruction and practice in these skills into the regular curriculum, in a sequence corresponding to Piaget's theory of children's cognitive maturation.

Barry K. Beyer (2) also distinguishes between "lower" (micro) and "higher" (macro) skills. The micro skills are *recall, comprehension, application, analysis, synthesis,* and *evaluation*. The macro processes are *problem solving* (following Michaelis's steps) and *decision making*, seen as problem solving geared to realize a predefined goal; *critical thinking* is seen as a synthesis of the two, but with criteria of its own—namely:

> ... distinguishing between verifiable facts and value claims; determining the reliability of a claim or source; determining the accuracy of a statement; distinguishing between warranted and unwarranted claims; distinguishing between relevant and irrelevant information, claims, or reasons; detecting bias; identifying stated and unstated assumptions; identifying ambiguous or equivocal claims or arguments; recognizing logical inconsistencies and determining the strength of an argument. (2, p. 555)

Beyer urges that educators create a program for skill instruction by focusing on (1) the operating procedures and accompanying rules for using that skill, (2) the effectiveness, adequacy, and appropriateness of each skill for a given context, and (3) the associated knowledge needed to make the skill operational. He suggests a curriculum in which students solve a problem and either, simultaneously describe or later analyze the steps they have taken in comparison with a model of "successful problem solving." Or the students might first be asked to apply a specific skill to a subject-related task, paying attention to the outcome; the teacher would then explain the skill in detail, exploring with the class the procedures used. During the next few weeks the students would engage in practice, while the teacher would elaborate on the skill, stressing new applications and components. Finally, the students would apply the skill again to subject-related goals.

The Learning to Learn system, developed by Marcia Heiman and Joshua Slomianko, focuses on what successful students actually *do* when mastering subject-matter material. In stressing an "internal dialogue" between learner and material, Heiman and Slomianko suggest a technique that they believe is fundamental to the critical thinking process (15, p. 7). Successful academic performers, consciously or unconsciously—

- ... ask questions of new materials, engaging in a covert dialogue with the author or listener, forming hypotheses, reading or listening for confirmation
- identify the component parts of complex principles and ideas, breaking down major tasks into smaller units
- devise informal feedback mechanisms to assess their own progress in learning
- focus on instructional objectives, identifying and directing their study behaviors to meet course objectives. (15, p. 16)

The core of the program is the students' generating of questions implicitly posed in a text or lecture, particularly those inquiring "how" or "why" rather than simply "what." When doing this, the learners come to grasp the significance of the dynamic interrelationships within the material being studied, while breaking down complex ideas and tasks into intellectually manageable parts. Students learn to rearrange these units to facilitate comparative analysis of the relationships among ideas; they then begin to see the patterns of the fields they are studying. As students become more familiar with the use of these strategies, they increasingly approximate the behavior of professionals in a given field—looking at the discipline from the viewpoint of the kinds of questions it asks, rather than as a set of unrelated ideas to be committed to memory. They begin to ask questions that go beyond the assigned material, and they are able to evaluate aspects of the field from both "professional" and personal, experiential perspectives. The role of the teacher is to provide instruction in the application of these skills to academic coursework.

Bloomfield College in New Jersey and Paul Robeson High School in Chicago also use the question-generating technique. This approach stresses the importance of an internal dialogue and the opportunity to obtain feedback. The focus is on the *person* who is studying and thinking. "Too often," William A. Sadler and Arthur Whimbey write, "students are not challenged to figure out how to use what they already know" (24). Using intuition, "students should be able to work from experience to new knowledge and competence" (24, p. 201). Participants in Bloomfield's Freshman Core Program are required to write argumentative papers for almost every class, which they then defend in seminars and workshops; in discussing assigned materials, they are encouraged to interject their own normative beliefs. At Robeson High School, students work in pairs, one as the problem solver and the second as the monitor, with the first defending his/her reasoning to the second. Attention is given to the creation of a supportive and motivating environment, small group settings, strong student/faculty relationships, dialogue, and tolerance of errors.

Another means of promoting student involvement in the thought-generating process is to set up hypothetical situations and ask students for their comments, analyses, or solutions. Edward deBono's CoRT system (Cognitive Research Trust) relies on a number of techniques, including a device he calls PMI (Plus, Minus, Interesting). Students are presented with a proposition; they then look for its "good" (plus) and "bad" (minus) points, as well as those points that are simply interesting (but neither good nor bad). The PMI, deBono notes, is "a scanning tool and not a judgment tool"; propositions are not related, and participants are allowed only two or three minutes to spend on each (8). He points out that the mere length of each list does not determine the worth of any alternative, and that reasoning is often subjective. This tool, which relates to Level 1 of deBono's complex system, is intended to induce "a general awareness of thinking as a skill" and to improve the student's "self-image" as a "thinker" (8, p. 708). Only on Level 2 is the participant introduced to "rational" problem solving in the sense we have been using.

Robert J. Sternberg (26) criticizes conventional problem-solving exercises as uninstructive because they are divorced from the real world in which students must live. In worldly situations the "problem" is often amorphous, contextual, amenable to certain answers, and fraught with important consequences. "Solutions" are often sought by groups, and on the basis of informal more than formal knowledge. Sternberg has designed a program, *Intelligence Applied*, which is intended to correct these flaws. Some of the sample problems Sternberg poses relate to public and political issues—for instance, the allocation of funds during a political campaign, the monitoring of compliance with an arms control treaty when the parties have a tendency to cheat, and the pollution by one state of a water supply on which two states are dependent. Participants—high school or college students of average ability—assume the roles of the persons involved in finding solutions. Other exercises involve the use of pictures, the meaning of which can be interpreted by identifying informal cues (body language, dress, age, socioeconomic class, etc.) (27).

Finally, there are programs that present the thinking process or the thought-inducing situation through the media. "Think-about," a videocassette series developed by the Agency for Instructional Television for middle-school learners, features formal techniques and problem presentation. Viewers are encouraged to approach a situation using a mnemonic: Hey, Wait! (realize and define the problem), Think (consider and experiment with alternatives), See (evaluate effectiveness), and So (consider further steps). According to Jerry L. Brown (3), the program has been effective in stimulating students to take actions in their own environments—e.g., they have created a newspaper, proposed changes in the menu in the cafeteria, and sought foster grandparents in a nursing home. Students have become highly motivated when presented with real problems they can actually attack.

The Public Broadcasting System's series "Why in the World," moderated by Walter Cronkite, has been used on the high school level to induce students to think critically about current events. Each program begins with a presentation of facts about a particular situation, followed by a discussion on the given topic between an expert and a group of students. The program itself can be analyzed in terms of the perspectives offered by the participants, the logic of the arguments, and the thoroughness with which the topic is explored. Using the program as a basis, the teacher can assign additional sources and further research, motivate students to speculate about future developments, and urge the assumption of positions following the scrutiny of individuals' own beliefs. The tool is intended both to develop thinking skills and to encourage "young people to become more thoughtfully involved in the world around them" (7).

As we have seen, there are a number of approaches to teaching thinking that are relevant to the social sciences. Some educators define thinking as a discrete process that must be mastered during a specified classroom time; others require the integration of techniques for teaching thinking skills into ongoing schedules and assignments. Some of the programs are themselves curriculums; others enrich what is usually being taught. Some can be used with any subject matter, and others relate to social studies as traditionally outlined. Some address the rational intellect, while others take into account more subjective factors such as intuition, personal experience, the learning environment, motivation, relationships, attachments, and self-image. Some rely on formal, structured exercises; others bring the dilemmas of practical life into the classroom; and still others turn the student toward the world. Most would improve students' classroom learning and their competence in reasoning and problem solving; one openly encourages them to seek to innovate within or change the surroundings in which they find themselves (3).

None, however, describes an ideal, but complete, classroom environment in which the expression of curiosity, active exploration, self-generated inquiry, problem solving, and creative/critical thinking become both the highest value and the norm.

A CLASSROOM ENVIRONMENT THAT PROMOTES THINKING

THE ENVIRONMENT

To suggest an abstract ideal, and then to set out to create it, might be seen as a fruitless and utopian task, especially when simpler reforms and measures can be carried out immediately. Restructuring schools anew was, of course, the goal of the free school movement that flourished in the United States in the 1960s and that is now regarded with considerable skepticism. The following ideas or questions, however, should be kept in mind when considering techniques and content within traditional settings:

1. *Self-confidence and self-image*: Do the students see themselves as active, able participants in the learning and thinking process? Whatever the task at hand, do they believe that it *can* be pursued by people such as they see themselves to be? Do they believe that *any* response they make to the material will be criticized as being inappropriate or simply wrong? Will they *not* speak up because nothing that they say will get an adequate hearing?

2. *Failure and success*: Does the class feel that it must mainly grasp and repeat the *one* right answer that will guarantee the highest grade? Is the receipt of grades the *main* task toward which the students orient themselves?

   Alternatively, are students afraid to try to grapple or work with the material for fear of failure? If they do think audaciously or intuitively, will they be penalized for these "errors"? Once a mistake is committed, is there any way in which it can be corrected? Will they be given credit for answers that, although not entirely "correct," can serve as a bridge for further thought?

3. *Relevance*: Does the material being studied have meaning for students' lives, and for the lives they will be leading? Is abstract material posed in such a way that it bears a human face, and a

dimension that is universal? Can students use their already acquired knowledge and understanding to continue learning?
4. *Relationship*: Is the class a truly cooperative and collective enterprise? Are the students and the teacher a resource and a source of feedback for one another? Is there sufficient trust that the students can go to one another, or to the teacher, for assistance or for comments on their ideas or projects? Alternatively, is the atmosphere so competitive that the success of one student means the failure of another?
5. *Fluidity*: Is the class schedule so organized that students have the time and ability to find the material they want, or to speak to the persons with whom they need to speak? Does the teacher facilitate such meetings and contacts if classroom time does not permit them? In scheduling assignments, is there room for false starts, further exploration, or merely cogitation? Alternatively, must the syllabus be covered and assignments handed in on time—no matter what? Must the students always (and rigidly) remain in the seats to which they have been assigned? Is it possible to *change* the classroom arrangement in accordance with the task at hand?
6. *Resources*: Are the students able to add to or borrow from classroom materials? Does the teacher bring in relevant source materials? Are the students encouraged to think of themselves, the teacher, and the wider community as sources of information for their projects? Can their projects be shared with other classes, parents, or the neighborhood? Do the students feel sufficiently empowered that *they*, by their own efforts, can procure resources or opportunities—say, a film or a trip—that the school itself cannot afford?
7. *"Doing" vs. "learning"*: Do class projects include—in addition to the mastery of material—a component in which an *activity* is carried out? Is the person or the environment *changed* as a result of this activity? Is the activity such that others, in or outside of the classroom, also receive some benefits? Does the project lead to a greater sense of personal efficacy and mastery? Does it draw attention to the skills and competence exhibited by the doer? Is the student directed to ways in which an activity can continue beyond the project's termination? Is the student shown that there is usually always *more* to do or learn?

8. *Ends*: Is the purpose of a component or assignment mainly academic or practical? Are students also made aware of an *ethical* or *moral* perspective in which options are choices bearing consequences? What do students *think* about the steps they have taken, or the methodology they have selected? Have they, in working with the material, learned more? Have they learned something about themselves? About others? Have they tapped the nonrational facilities of their minds—their abilities to imagine, to feel, to speculate at random, to daydream?

By setting up these criteria, a teacher creates a bias in favor of active, empowering, cooperative, exploratory, and open-ended education, tailored, at least in part, to the needs, interests, and backgrounds of the students being taught. But regardless of the educational philosophy embraced, it is important to address and discuss students' feelings about their own worth and value, either as a separate course or topic, or during regular activities. People trapped in their own sense of futility and powerlessness will not easily commit themselves to an attempt at mastery because, in their own eyes, failure is foreordained. As two parent/teacher founders of an Orange County, California, elementary school program, Project Self-Esteem, noted: "The child who likes himself learns better. You can't teach a child who thinks he's dumb" (17). Even if no such program or curriculum exists, the teacher can bolster a student's self-esteem by—

- Actively listening to a student's response in a nonjudgmental manner;
- Reinforcing the positive in what is being said;
- Acknowledging each student's comments, even if they are "wrong" or likely to be misdirecting;
- Exploring the implications of a remark, so that the students themselves will renounce or correct an inappropriate position;
- Suggesting that the students themselves verify or explain their statements;
- Giving students a task that might involve a "correction" of the earlier "mistake";
- Posing an idea opposite to that which the student has expressed, and then asking the student what she/he thinks and why;

- Encouraging *any* goal, no matter how unrealistic in the teacher's eyes, that the student has indicated a willingness to pursue, and then discussing with the student what steps should be taken to meet this goal;
- Establishing rules for class discussion that, for any reason, exclude personal attacks and provide for common courtesy;
- Rephrasing a remark in a way that gives it the greatest possible credence, and then opening up the question for general discussion, pro and con;
- Making oneself available to students who desire to discuss their problems or their feelings;
- Personally complimenting any student who, contrary to his/her usual pattern, has done unexpectedly able work, including an invitation to more personal discussion or consultation, should the student wish it; and
- Allowing a student, through redone or additional assignments, to recoup much of the ground or points that have been lost through error or carelessness.

Students are ultimately responsible for *what* they learn, but the task of the teacher and the classroom is to produce good learners. As Neil Postman and Charles Weingartner (22) have pointed out, good learners have confidence in their own abilities; enjoy solving problems; know what is relevant to their own survival; have a healthy respect for fact, yet rely on their own judgments, are flexible; are not afraid of being "wrong"; and often take time in coming up with answers.

If, as Postman and Weingartner also suggest, the learning environment has four critical components—"the learner, the teacher, the 'to-be-learned' and the strategies for learning" (22, p. 51)—the setting *and* the general approach should be chosen so as to maximize their intermeshing in an active sense.

THE METHODOLOGY

There is, of course, no single methodology or teaching strategy that suffices for all grades or all occasions. However, some are more useful than others in catalyzing the thinking process.

One effective approach is the *inquiry method* (22). Through this method, all lessons are posed to students as a *problem* (e.g., Why was there a Civil War?). While the teacher acts as one of the questioners, she or he is primarily a facilitator. The focus is not so much on the questions that he/she asks and that the students answer, but on how the students interact among themselves. Care is taken *not* to sum up what is being said or simply to "cover" a given body of material. Rather, the next task or lesson evolves from the direction the current discussion takes.

For instance, one student might suggest slavery as a cause of the Civil War. The question might then be raised as to what the objections to that institution were, and why—at that time or now. The discussion might examine racism, prejudice, and equal rights and opportunities, or the rights of states and communities to determine their way of life without interference from a central government, or how important an issue has to be for people to take up arms and fight. Then students might be asked to draw up a position statement or to present a report. Again, the emphasis would be on the reasoned argument or feelings expressed, rather than on recall. Facts would be used to buttress the arguments.

Another technique appropriate to such a lesson would be role playing. Students could be asked, either on an impromptu basis or after research, to assume the following roles: a slave or a slaveholder, soldiers (or parents of soldiers) from the North and the South, an abolitionist, and a states-rights senator. After the actors present their reactions, the other students, as members of an audience with a contemporary point of view, would pose questions for them to answer.

With both techniques, the teacher would focus on the dialogue that is taking place (again, largely among the students) and on class behavior. For instance:

- Are all students participating?
- Are the students challenging each other? With what frequency and conviction?
- Are the arguments becoming more detailed and sophisticated?
- Is critical thinking—the willingness to suspend judgment in anticipation of facts, to use facts in support of judgment, to alter initial opinions, and to tolerate ambiguity, etc.—going on, even though the students may not recognize the process?
- Where do the students want the class to go from here?

If the class remains largely passive, or erupts into intolerance, it can be asked to analyze itself.

When these extroverted techniques are used, some students may be too shy and self-conscious to reveal their ideas in front of their classmates. Others may play for the audience or the approval of the teacher, saying only what is fashionable or acceptable. For these reasons, teachers should be wary of grading performance, or of using such events as material for any test except to develop, or futher solidify, a student's own reactions.

There are ways, of course, that such dialogues can be developed in greater anonymity. For instance, students can present their arguments as essays, or as contributions to a collective class newspaper; opinions can be revealed through the circulation of a questionnaire or ballot, followed by discussion of results. Nonetheless, if refuge is taken behind a piece of paper, much of the spontaneity of oral interaction is lost.

LEARNING SOCIAL SCIENCE: THE CURRICULUM, GRADE BY GRADE

THE PRIMARY SCHOOL EXPERIENCE

It should be remembered that children enter school as thinking beings. They also come with experience that is largely *social*—concerning themselves, other people, and their environment. School may appear to some as an alien environment, a place of little relevance in which they are imprisoned until their release in the afternoon when they take up their "real life" once again. Such a dichotomy should be avoided. Rather, the school should become another arena of life to which children can take events happening elsewhere and be treated seriously, and in which they acquire the skills, stamina, and self-confidence to venture more broadly and deeply into their surroundings.

Therefore, in the primary grades—or at least in the earliest grades—there is no social studies per se or, rather, little subject matter that isn't social. Almost any lesson—from mathematics to reading, to explicit units on the family, neighborhood professions, and the like—can be used to teach children about the world.

Learning also should draw upon children's basic (and already developed) skills—their abilities to see, to observe, to listen, to talk, and to draw; their propensities to ask questions, to make statements, and to collect objects. It should also use children's tendencies to daydream, imagine, and play.

Concern has been expressed about reading achievement levels, and whether word recognition or phonics is the appropriate approach. What is often forgotten in this debate is that written material is just ordinary language set down and preserved on paper. Children will most likely *want* to read if they are interested in the information encoded, and they will *learn* to read more and more fluently by constantly attempting it. It also might be helpful if students' own words are what is being read. As long as reading is not presented as a precipice to scale—and an impossible, tiring, and embarrassing one at that—the teacher will eventually be able to use books as part of a social studies curriculum. Until then, however, there are faculties that can be used in place of literacy.

The teacher should stress, for the youngest child, the importance of *environment*. Above all, the children must see the classroom as a natural place in which to spend their time. That is, students might be encouraged to make it their second home, to identify their own space or corner, and to bring their own things, mementos, and decorations. It is impossible and impractical in most institutions to turn—as the free school movement once imagined—each classroom into a clubhouse, complete with rug, armchairs, TV, library, and kitchen. Nonetheless, space can be found for—

- Photos of the children and their families;
- Collections of inexpensive items and materials;
- Drawings;
- Cutouts from newspapers and magazines; and
- Games and other small possessions—including animals that can be cared for—that the children want to share.

It is usual to set up such exhibits as part of a project or in celebration of an event or a season. However, they need not be that formal or planned. A teacher might experiment by allowing decorations at any time, or in almost any nonobstructive place, *at a child's own initiative*. In this way the children are able to express themselves and show how they view their surroundings.

As mentioned earlier, children are almost always ready to comment, to supply an oral history. The role of the teacher is to find an object or a topic through which such thoughts are catalyzed. Children already see themselves as actors in the center of their universe, and they have ideas about what that universe is like—and how it ought to be. Therefore, the goal is to expand that world view and to have it shared. Immediate topics that come to mind are these:

- Parents, families
- Friendship
- Work
- Routines (food, clothing, etc.)
- Television and other types of entertainment
- Emotions
- Religious and ethnic heritage
- Neighborhood, town and city.

Recent books by psychologist Robert Coles (5, 6) reveal that children in the primary grades also have a moral and political life, however much derived from parents. Thus, even before the advent of true literacy, materials concerning current events and personalities can be brought to class for discussion. Some lead-ins might be—

- What would you do if . . . ?
- What do you feel about . . . ?
- How did you react to . . . ?
- What should . . . do about . . . ?
- How was this shown on television?

Disturbing events or phenomena (nuclear weapons, wars, disasters, etc.) are less so to children once they have been broached, and feelings and information shared under the guidance of a sympathetic teacher. Discussions of current topics can also serve as a springboard for projects on affected countries, peoples, groups, and phenomena.

Using a tape recorder, a child's spoken thoughts and reveries can be recorded and played back. Such words can also be transcribed, revealing the connection between the spoken and the written word. Sylvia Ashton-Warner, a New Zealand primary school teacher, taught Maori students to read by asking them to suggest a key vocabulary of personally important words; she then wrote down these words for the children to master (1). A similar group of words can be drawn from discussion lessons that fall in the realm of social studies. Discussion lessons can also be enhanced by having students create drawings, poems, or imaginative stories (again, presented orally and written down by the teacher if the children lack the necessary skills).

The teacher can particularly look to art as an early and expressive "language" because, as Coles points out, children can often draw what they cannot yet say or think (5). Thus, during a unit on the family, the class can be asked to—

- Draw a happy scene;
- Draw something that made you sad;
- Draw something that happened last Sunday;
- Draw whatever you would like your family to do or to have, if you could make a wish that would come true; and
- Draw yourself, and any of your friends, as you come home from school.

The pictures can then be displayed in sequence, or as a panorama. Through interpretation (What are they doing? What is taking place here?), the class can begin to think about a *common* experience, as well as what has been individually expressed.

Pre-operational Stage (to age 7)

In Piaget's pre-operational stage (from birth to age seven), children's mental focus is very much on what appears before their eyes. Therefore, attempts might be made to use material that can be seen, touched, tasted, heard, or otherwise experienced. The teacher might bring role models from the community (the policeperson, fireperson, auto mechanic, shopkeeper, etc.) complete with uniform and tools, into the classroom so that children can hear about and see what they do for a living. Also, the teacher might take the class on field trips into the community to visit places of work and service. The class can be helped to make something for outside persons (residents of an old age home, hospital patients, children at a preschool center), or to receive something from them (sweets, a souvenir, a booklet, scrap materials, etc.). In the classroom the children can recreate what they have seen or the places they have visited, and in certain instances they can establish ongoing relationships (with the aged, with the very young, or with adults who are interested).

Operational Stage (ages 7 to 11)

By the time students reach the operational stage—from age seven to eleven—they should be sufficiently skilled in reading to handle an appropriate social studies textbook. However, the text should not restrict the boundaries of what is to be explored; rather it should be a springboard for further inquiry. Heiman and Slomianko (15) suggest one method directed toward textual and subject-matter mastery: declarative statements—e.g., "The development of agriculture changed the pattern of human settlement"—are turned into questions that ask "how" and "why"—i.e., "How did agriculture change the way in which people lived? Why did it do this?" A second strategy is to call forth identification and empathy with the group of persons being studied, no matter how distant in time and space. Role-playing exercises such as the following fall into this category:

- Imagine that you are . . . ?

- What if you met . . . today?
- What reactions would you have if you visited . . . ?
- What do you like/dislike about . . . ?
- What can we learn from . . . ?

Students can respond in essay, dramatic, oral or pictorial form.

Students at this age can use the community as the field for a "treasure hunt" for classifiable material; the objects can either be brought into the classroom and categorized and recategorized according to their uses, or simply be "sighted" by a team. The team that is quickest, most accurate, or most imaginative might win a prize. Following are some possible themes that would require student speculation:

- Things that were in use when your mother/father was a girl/boy
- Things that could be found in England, Egypt, or whatever country the class is studying
- Things that are likely to be there in the year 2000
- Things that are necessary for life
- Things that should be taken to a desert island, on a trip, in an emergency, etc.

Collections might be made ancillary to projects, or models or mechanisms built.

Postman (21) suggests that in this era of ubiquitous television, in which programs bearing no relation to one another succeed each other every thirty minutes, and channels can be changed at will, lessons should be linked through a recurring theme. He stresses the importance of "unity and continuity of human experience and feeling"—which is exactly what social studies is all about. The units being studied in the upper elementary grades can be linked—

- By chronological order, so that one development is shown to be conditioned by the previous one;
- By functional order, so that one activity is seen as impacting on or complementary to another; and
- As examples of the use of human faculties to bring order to the world (writing, tool making, etc.).

Teachers should not hesitate to introduce material *not* in the syllabus—a poem, a story, music, an advertisement, or a newspaper clipping—even if it is not expressly aimed at a young audience, if they feel that this material is provocative, appropriate, relevant, and would not seem offensive to the students. Students can be urged to do the same. Much of the material students are likely to present might relate to the popular culture—i.e., comic books, celebrities, pop music, reports on TV shows, jokes, and the like. If the teacher can be sympathetic to and respectful of the students' tastes, these materials and activities might be added to the class agenda because they reflect the students' thinking and interests.

Teachers should also keep an open mind toward the assignment of TV shows or movies as required class assignments, if they are relevant to what is being studied and if all members of the class have access to them. Children in the upper elementary and middle school grades are often strongly attached to "heroes" in the popular culture; and, by using these real or fictitious personalities as a shield, they may be able to think about themselves and social situations in ways that they might not otherwise be willing to attempt. Movies and TV shows can also be useful in developing exercises on *moral judgment*. Thus, students can be asked:

- Are the characters good or bad?
- Is the ending happy or sad, realistic or unrealistic?
- Are the characters likable or not, and why?
- With whom did the students identify or empathize?
- What was the problem or point of the show?
- What would the student have done in a character's place?

Some television shows, of course, are directly educational; they communicate easily through sounds and pictures what students still can obtain only with difficulty from books. Movies or videotapes are usually welcomed by students—if only as a break from the usual routine. These media materials, if appropriately selected, can be a teaching asset. Yet, they should not be allowed to contribute to student passivity. Like the textbook, field trip, and project, television and the movies can stimulate thinking and futher inquiry, *if* the teacher insists on this and points the way.

THE MIDDLE/JUNIOR HIGH SCHOOL YEARS: DEVELOPMENTAL CONSIDERATIONS

During the middle school years, social studies is regarded as a separate subject, with an instructor to teach it and a particular classroom in which it is taught. Students range in age from eleven to fourteen or fifteen; that is, they are preadolescents and adolescents who are experiencing physical, psychological, and behavioral changes. Individuals vary according to their particular chronological and developmental positions on this age continuum; in one class there are persons still immersed in childhood sitting side by side with others who have the characteristics of teenagers. For these reasons these grades may be extremely difficult to teach.

On the one hand, these adolescents are able to carry out formal operations; they can grasp general concepts, reason, make deductions, undertake comparisons, and formulate generalizations—the core of critical thinking—without being limited to first-hand experience. They can understand ideas such as time, distance, and space, and can draw or construct more or less accurate graphs, maps, charts, models, and diagrams. Their attention spans increase, as do their problem-solving abilities and their capacity for concentrated independent study. Reading is no longer problematic (or should not be). Thus, the teaching of social studies takes on a larger scope, and the teacher can work with many more tools and options.

On the other hand, these students live in the shadow of peer approval and under the influence of the popular culture, both of which are frequently anti-intellectual. Relationships with the opposite sex and love/hate friendships with the same sex may be particularly tense. The teacher, therefore, might spend a lot of time simply keeping order and diverting students' attention from their more social interests. Students often rebel against the teacher simply because he/she is in a position of authority; rather than saying what they personally feel or think, students might express opinions accepted by their peers. Adolescents and pre-adolescents have been found to be simultaneously extremely idealistic (yet critical) and extraordinarily self-centered (yet insecure). At times, working with them can require the skills of the psychologist more than those of the educator.

Thus, the tactful approach mentioned earlier is particularly appropriate. Above all, the teacher must avoid exposing students to public embarrassment and engaging in a test of wills. The latter is at times hard to avoid because some students are constantly testing limits, and the teacher must set some, lest the classroom become chaotic. Some teachers are able to gain students' attention through an entertaining teaching style, while others possess personal characteristics that command respect. The firmest ground, however, lies in the establishment of a personal working relationship of trust and limited friendship, in which the teacher understands the student's needs and abilities, yet directs her/his energies toward effort and achievement. By this time, some students are already using assumptions based on sex, race, and class to define their personal and academic horizons; others are working to overcome such assumptions. While some schools segregate the achievers from the nonachievers, others do not —if only because few academically oriented individuals can be found. In some surroundings, sexuality and pregnancy, drug abuse, truancy, and crime—and their prevention—may be of immediate concern. (These issues fall under the general heading of "social studies," although not in the state-prescribed curriculum.) It is possible, however, to unite students with divergent interests and ambitions around two common identities—those of the *individual* and the *citizen*.

Curriculum Focus: The Student as an Individual and a Citizen

An emphasis on the student as an individual and a citizen is congruent with state-mandated social studies curriculums, which usually introduce the student to Western (sometimes world) civilizations and to American culture, history, and government. Concepts, themes, and goals are drawn from the various social science disciplines.

For instance, emphasis on the individual might begin with a generalization on *efficacy*: the individual's ability to imagine, describe, control, and change her or his natural and social environment. Some connecting ideas, themes, and questions might be these:

- How is individuality defined in any given culture?
- How is this definition the same as, or different from, the beliefs of contemporary Americans?
- What relationships are established among individuals and groups: family, kin, class, tribe, faith, state, etc.?
- What are the society's goals and ideals? What are its "goods"? In which form or medium are these goals and ideals expressed?
- Does the society desire change in itself and its environment?
- What tools and techniques are used? Are they individually or collectively invented?
- Do individuals see themselves as able to alter their status and environment, or are these ascribed?
- To what extent do individuals feel in control of their lives on a daily basis?

- Through which ideas, forms, or institutions might people gain their sense of meaning and belonging?

Although students of this age are usually capable of thinking in a distant context, they may not be *motivated* to do so; a society or era they have never seen holds little interest. Therefore, a reference point for discussion might be their *own* sense of efficacy and individuality with the goal of empowerment and self-awareness. As mentioned earlier, students become more interested in mastering a unit when they see that it leads to something that they can *do* or *change*. Therefore, they might be stimulated to take action—i.e., to express their sense of individuality and efficacy in a contructive manner—within their school or their wider community, if they have the opportunity to discuss or participate in programs dealing with the social problems that may plague it. Such opportunities might include the following:

- Organizing schoolwide discussion groups
- Organizing a lecture series
- Organizing or participating in peer counseling, tutoring, a Big Brother program, or other service
- Conducting a clean-up drive
- Joining a community, church, or recreational organization
- Planning school functions.

If the teacher is willing to *assist* students in such projects, the class's confidence in the teacher's interest can only increase.

The students, however, should not be allowed to remain entirely self-centered. Therefore, exercises that allow them to project themselves into another's place are useful. If students have access to school and public libraries, reference materials, and, in some cases, a second language, these exercises—whether resulting in reports, essays, or projects—become more sophisticated. On the basis of research, carried out singly or in groups, students would be able to do the following:

- Explain a situation using the ideas and assumptions of the culture being studied
- Solve a problem as someone of that culture might do it
- Criticize that culture as would a visitor—i.e., an American—and defend it as would a native

- Write an autobiography as if one were living at the place or during that time
- Conduct a debate between a native of the culture and a visitor.

Any consideration of American culture, history, and government involves the concepts of democracy *and* citizenship. Unlike the consideration of past or foreign societies, the subject matter here is not merely academic because this society is where students will most likely live, work, and vote.

Any analysis of American institutions and government should be objective, with room for differing interpretations. Nonetheless, both teachers and students should approach the subject from deeply rooted normative perspectives which, in the students' case, may be largely unexamined and divorced from facts. There is the need to convey information not only for itself, but also for its usefulness in terms of rights and duties. It might also be desirable, in respect to the nation and the students' place in it, to make implicit values, goals, and ideals explicit and open to discussion. At times this can mean defining or redefining terminology (What is democracy? What is *a* democracy? What is a republic? A people?). It can require investigation of the ideal itself (Is democracy possible?), or of its pursuit (How have Americans attempted to create a more democratic society?). Finally, students can pass a judgment or make an evaluation (Does the United States have a truly democratic society?).

Applying principles or ideals to problem-solving situations will probably reveal that the path from ideals to implementation might not be as straight as previously imagined. For example:

- What if, in the name of free speech, someone fraudulently yells "fire" in a crowded room?
- What if someone publishes a recipe for committing suicide (or making nuclear weapons) in a free press?
- Is it all right for someone to practice a religion that allows for seven wives (or husbands)?

Such questions can lead to discussions that weigh the rights of others against the rights of self.

American history and politics provide ample opportunities for simulations. Events that might be re-enacted by students include the Continental Congress, the Lincoln–Douglas debates, any nominating convention, and, of course, any election campaign currently under way. Students might take straw votes, hold moot courts, and conduct sessions of the legislature. Afterward, the strategies and maneuvers the students actually used might be discussed.

Finally, the teacher might bring a lesson on the democratic process into the classroom. The class might be asked to—

- Write a constitution,
- Elect its officers,
- Set up rules of order and operation,
- Create an agenda,
- Assign tasks and duties,
- Define jurisdiction,
- Raise general questions,
- Hold debates,
- Set up voting procedures and take questions to a vote, and
- Pass resolutions.

The teacher would establish the framework and basic rules for the exercise so that the students could be self-managing, and would serve as referee—in addition to any more direct role she/he might assume. Again, the students would discuss, either periodically or at the end of the exercise, what had been taking place.

Students at the middle/junior high school level can be expected to read a newspaper. They can also follow broad outlines of the news on television and radio. Student discussions of current events—joined to regular subject matter units or held at times expressly set aside for them—can be expected to be deeper, and more complex, than those occurring in the primary grades. Students should now be able to focus on issues, personalities, evaluations, and feelings. Members of particular ethnic, religious, racial, or gender groups might find some topics to be of particular importance to them. If they are given the opportunity to express their specific viewpoints, these discussions might be broadened to include a particular group's contributions to American society and politics in general. If the class (or school) is polarized along group lines, it is vital that students from diverse backgrounds understand each other's thinking. Often stereotypes persist for lack of information to the contrary.

Students can also now take a more critical look at the media, particularly television, the movies, and home video cassettes. A unit or group of sessions on the media might include a look at the kind of communication each medium is intended to make, as well as an analysis of material

communicated. Some categories that might be used are as follows:
- Oral versus written
- Pictures versus words
- Passive versus active
- Mass versus individual
- Private versus public
- An appeal to the heart versus the mind
- Commercial versus nonprofit
- Mass versus elite
- Solitary versus cooperative
- Localized versus unconnected to any particular time or space.

Again, the focus would be on thinking *about* the media and their effects on users and viewers, rather than on producing any defined fit. Students might then turn to any media artifact and look for its *bias* (intellectual, emotional, political, social, sensory, etc.).

Integrating Thinking Skills into the Curriculum

Earlier the question was raised as to whether thinking skills should be taught explicitly or simply carried out. A similar dilemma would be whether skiers should receive instruction and practice in technique before strapping on their skis, or be allowed to try their native skills on a gentle slope where they could not get hurt too easily or too seriously. My own bias is toward the latter, for several reasons.

First of all, the delight is often in the doing or, as in Moliere's play in which a character finds out he has been speaking prose, in naming what one has in fact been doing all along. Second, instruction in technique is likely to be regarded as another exercise by both the academically and the nonacademically inclined, something to be forgotten once the unit is finished or, even worse, ignored along with all other "lessons." Third, even the most conscientious student is unlikely to consult a handbook or manual, or refer back to (the memorized) "seven easy steps," every time she/he tries to think. The goal of exercises in critical thinking is to take what has been practiced *in* the classroom *out* of it for application to daily life. It is ultimately to create—or educate—a perceptive, curious, and conscious (and self-conscious) personality. Too much emphasis on methodology and technique, on being "right" or "correct," can lead to the kind of self-consciousness—overcautiousness in approach and fear of failure, not to mention avoidance of the task—that educators do not want.

Yet, from the point of view of the teacher, an emphasis on spontaneity will most likely require a trade-off. Students' performance in thinking exercises, especially in the lower middle/junior high school grades, can be rather awkward, or very poor indeed. Often their statements will be simplistic, their arguments nonsequential, and their factual data wrong. Some students will not have done preparatory homework, some will not understand the "rules" of any game or, if they do, will not follow them. The same points will have to be repeated, time and time again. While some students will dominate the proceedings—sometimes in a disruptive manner—others will spend more time looking out of the window rather than observing, must less participating in, an exercise. In short, the teacher's patience and tolerance might be sorely tried, and the schedule for covering the syllabus or for preparing the class for quantitative examinations thrown off track. Therefore, individual teachers must decide on the particular balance between mastery of the curriculum and exploration of the implications of the subject matter, with a lesser emphasis on outcomes, that suits their situations.

There are, of course, steps that teachers can take to reduce the chaos level or—more positively—to improve the level of student performance.

1. Prepare students for the factual matter that they will be handling. This can mean holding an exercise after a unit has been taught or having them engage in extensive preparatory research and homework, which is carefully checked.
2. Be aware of the formal steps of logical analysis, even though the students themselves might not have studied them directly. In this way the students' responses can be rephrased or turned in a more analytical direction, generalizations and clichés broken down, and additional questions raised.
3. Post guidelines for the thinking process in the classroom where they can be easily seen, and/or distribute them to students in the form of handbills or data sheets. Such guidelines can be simplified in the form suggested by "Thinkabout" (3):
    - *Hey, Wait!*—What is the problem?
    - *Think*—What are your alternatives?
    - *See*—What results are you getting?
    - *So*—What more do you need?
4. Allow students access to notes and other reference materials, and provide time during larger group projects for them to pause,

caucus, consult, and check. If necessary, a session can be recessed, to be resumed after additional data have been gathered.

5. Explicitly go over the rules of the exercise before you begin, and review them periodically. This might include a statement of exactly what is being graded and what ends are sought.

6. Intervene in the dialogue or discussion, but in a nonthreatening and nonjudgmental manner, with the aim of clarifying or elaborating on what has been said, rather than refuting it. Such interventions can include—
   - Is this what you mean by . . . ?
   - You seem to be telling us . . . ?
   - Do all . . . always . . . ?
   - Maybe . . . sometimes does not . . . ?
   - Would . . . also meet this criterion?

7. Present problems that you or the class is having with an exercise to the class for its consideration as soon as possible after they are recognized. Then ask the students what they want to do about them.

   It is useful to avoid direct criticism of other people's actions or performance ("you" statements). Instead, use "I" statements:
   - It seems to me that . . .
   - I have noticed that . . .
   - I am having trouble with . . .
   - I am disturbed or disappointed that . . .

   By asking the class to speak, you can determine the degree to which one student's objection is more generally shared. As much as possible, the class should suggest its own remedies (more care in preparing outside of class, more decorum, greater attentiveness to the exercise or to the rules of order, etc.).

8. Be available for consultation. Such meetings might be held before or after the school day, before or after the class period, or during sessions expressly set aside for them. Consultation can be at the students' request, or required, at set intervals and times for all participants.

   Students will be more willing to seek advice on preparation and performance if they are told—and feel—that you are a resource, if they are involved in the project, and if they are desirous of a given reward or end (feedback, a grade, etc.).

9. Have the class itself review what has taken place during the exercise. Aspects to review might include the following:
   - The dynamics of any interaction
   - Processes of critical thinking displayed
   - The extent and patterns of participation
   - Results achieved, and questions answered
   - Conclusions to be drawn
   - Questions still to be answered
   - Suggestions for improvement
   - Benefits derived
   - Whether any spin-off projects can be carried out or the subject pursued in another form.

10. Allow for a "second chance" or improved performance through demonstrated work. While students must learn that *some* adherence to schedules, deadlines, guidelines, and other requirements is necessary, these should not unnecessarily confine the thinking and learning processes. It is better that a student learn from an error, or make amends for carelessness, than to suffer penalties for errors that cannot be corrected.

11. In speculative exercises, regard the "journey" rather than "arrival" as the most important product. Hence, students should be rewarded or complimented as much—if not more—for daring, curiosity, audaciousness, effort, involvement, and improved (mental and participatory) behavior as for being easily and safely "right" or "orthodox." While the mechanics of spelling, grammar, handwriting, etc., add to a performance's appeal, their absence may not entirely detract from or destroy its content. Faulty mechanics certainly need correction, but they should not downgrade the value of other kinds of input.

Especially if this is the students' initial contact with critical and creative thinking, teachers should have modest expectations of students in the middle grades. Quality and content will often be much lower than teachers might imagine if they performed similar exercises themselves—and much inferior to what the students themselves might produce later on at the high school level. Nonetheless, if age and inexperience are factored into evaluation, issues and projects should not be rejected because they are regarded as too difficult or too advanced. Thinking and creativity, after all, are processes that improve with practice. It is better that students glimpse their own potentials than not to know that these potentials exist.

THE HIGH SCHOOL YEARS: DEVELOPMENTAL CONSIDERATIONS

The differences between the high school and the junior high/middle school are less significant than are those between the latter and the elementary school. In many localities, enrollment decreases through attrition; the remaining population is more sharply differentiated between the college- and the employment-bound (and, for the former, between those seeking admission to competitive and noncompetitive institutions). In the higher grades, some students will have assumed the responsibilities of young adults in terms of work, family, and other rights and privileges; future opportunities for employment, career specialization, and marriage are very much on their minds. Seeing themselves as already developed personalities and individuals—the reality sometimes to the contrary—high school students have a strong desire to be treated as such. They are also more prepared to assert their individuality and opinions in the classroom than are their younger brothers and sisters.

High school students are also able to comprehend material that has been prepared for an adult audience. This gives all students access to secondary source material, newspapers, magazines, and reference works; the most able can handle classic works of thought and literature. Depending on the level and the inclinations of a class, the teacher is able to assign supplementary or independent reading, along with the required school-supplied text.

Social Studies as an Academic Discipline

In some states social studies is a wholly or partially "required" subject; in others it is an elective, with students retaining considerable latitude in the courses they take. Some students select their program in the field with a view to passing or scoring well on certain examinations (state examinations, advanced placement examinations, College Board achievement tests, etc.). At one time social studies was synonymous with history (American, European, etc.), and some of that structure has been preserved. On the other hand, some schools now make available offerings in economics, sociology, anthropology, geography, psychology, political science, and great ideas, in addition to history, and include in the social studies curriculum such alternatives as marriage and the family, consumer education, and human sexuality.

In any case, what is new at the high school level is the presentation of the concept of a *discipline*—that is, the collection, study, and analysis of data on a limited kind of human activity from a particular (and supposedly objective) perspective. Thus, students study not only that activity segment (the economy, government, etc.) but also what professionals have concluded about it, along with the latter's methodologies and concerns. Even in courses that are geographical-area oriented (Europe, the Soviet Union, the Third World, etc.) and, therefore, more comprehensive, the contributions of the various disciplines, or their institutionalized methods of analysis, can be taken into account.

As a discipline, social studies is a particular way of focusing on patterns of behavior and attitudes, which may or may not be shared by lay people. For example, economists look at output, costs, prices, sales, and profits; they also look at labor, firms, sectors, and cycles. In addition, economics is a language because it involves a new way of naming and describing phenomena.

High school students should learn to understand and begin to use the language and tools of the particular social science they are studying. In that way, they can think about familiar phenomena (the family or the firm) in a more sophisticated way.

Instruction cannot be so dry that it turns into an academic exercise, nor so commonplace that it dampens the interest of students who might be considering that discipline as a college major or career. Once major definitions or concepts have been introduced, one way to strike a balance is to have students function as if they were professionals approaching a body of material. For instance, students can—

- Take a relevant newspaper article (or magazine clipping, feature story, etc.); underline all the terms and concepts they can find; paraphrase those that are written in common language; and summarize, from a disciplinary point of view, what the article is about; or

- Write up an autobiographical sketch or scenario (about work, dating, budgeting, family relationships, personal behavior) in ordinary language; and then rewrite or analyze the sketch from a disciplinary point of view, using newly introduced concepts and language.

The students might report on or analyze such material *solely* as if they were professionals receiving it as data, taking into consideration the following questions:

- What is the subject under discussion?
- What questions does the author raise?
- What key concepts are we looking for?
- What questions can we, as analysts, raise?
- What can be concluded?
- What can be questioned?
- What are other potential points of comparison and inquiry?

Using such exercises as source material, students might develop a dictionary, worksheets, or a simple textbook for classroom use.

Novels, short stories, movies, television programs, and other kinds of fictional material can also be employed in revealing the tension between commonplace and professional considerations. After reading or viewing the material, students can first discuss problems and conflicts from the point of view of the characters (what they did or would say, do, feel), and then they can examine the characters and context from the point of view of a practitioner—e.g., a sociologist, political scientist, or psychologist.

Finally, students might undertake a task performed by professionals in the discipline. For example, they could—

- "Buy" and manage a portfolio of stocks for a period of time with the aim of increasing capital; teams could select and track their portfolios and trade with other teams;
- Chart leading economic indicators and make performance predictions, over the quarter or for the coming year;
- Conduct a public opinion poll concerning voters' attitudes on candidates and issues, and analyze the results;
- Administer simple psychological tests to a sample population, or draw up in-depth psychological profiles for selected subjects, including, perhaps, the self;
- Make a sociological analysis of a segment of the community or the school; or
- Follow, over time, developments in a particular country with a view toward predicting what will shortly happen there.

Sometimes it is possible to ground such exercises in actual experience. Possible alternative activities include forming a simple business or service company, organizing a fund-raising drive, conducting campaigns for school office or on school issues, and serving "internships" within the home community.

High school students should be more adept at role playing, problem solving, and simulations than are younger students. In addition to carrying out the projects suggested earlier, they would be able to—

- Hold an interdisciplinary panel on a given issue, with each member approaching the topic as a member of a profession would;
- Hold a similar panel on which *each* member was an "expert," with the goal of reaching conclusions on the case;
- Make a presentation for the class to analyze;
- Simulate and role-play such events as a corporate board meeting, a terrorist attack, a Soviet–American nuclear crisis confrontation, or intervention with a troubled youth;
- Solve an international situation in such a way that none of the countries involved is annihilated in a war; or
- Bring a troubled family together.

The emphasis here would be on understanding and dealing with differing and/or conflicting perspectives, purposes, interests, and criteria, and on reconciling these in a compromise, solution, or approach that might work. High schools also have access to such formal "modeling" programs as the Model United Nations and those simulating the activities of the national and state governments.

It is important, too, for students to subject the discipline they are studying and its own implicit assumptions to an analytical critique. This can at times be accomplished by looking *positively* at phenomena or developments that are commonly thought of as dysfunctional and/or heretical. An example might be a society in which—

- People do *not* work for economic gain (but from other motives) or do not work at all;
- All students do not have to go to school;
- There is a one-party, dictator system;
- Marriage is *not* the norm; or

- Religion is denigrated.

The aim of such discussion would be not to advocate such alternatives, but rather to grasp their logic and coherency (if any) and to determine if they are somehow excluded or condemned by a discipline's way of thinking. It is an exercise designed to correct for bias.

Alternatively, teachers can ask their students to list what they believe are a discipline's spoken and implicit assumptions. These can then be tested for accuracy, comprehensiveness, usefulness, etc. Students can be asked to determine if these assumptions apply to all, some, or most of the items in a particular class or category, and whether they hold up against the students' own experiences. Assumptions that do not pass these tests can be qualified or discarded.

A Focus of Instruction: Ethical and Normative Issues

The high school years are the final opportunity for educators to introduce ethical and normative considerations. This kind of analysis is important for a number of reasons. First, such personal standards are necessary for adolescents going out into the world; second, we need to have "good"—i.e., thoughtful—citizens; and, finally, students are by now developed moral beings, they have an interest in ethical issues that touch their lives, and they are capable of handling ideas with which they might *a priori* disagree.

Should teachers present their own norms and values, or those representing a community consensus? It is perhaps best that teachers *not* hide behind a veil of impartiality and objectivity. More positively, teachers *should* state their own biases, provided that this is done *explicitly*—e.g., "I personally believe, or support . . . " "Many people think . . . " A clear demarcation should be made between the teacher's beliefs and the students' rights to formulate their own attitudes, choosing from the whole range of options available. In holding such discussions, it might be desirable for the teacher to—

1. Outline what is being graded: the opinion *or* arguments in its defense. In almost every circumstance, the former should not be graded, no matter how obnoxious or disturbing. Instead, the criteria (veracity of supporting data, consistency, acceptance of consequences, etc.) by which the quality of a supporting argument can be assessed should be clearly defined.

2. Caution against accepting or repeating the opinion of the teacher (or any authority) simply on the basis of authority or fear of consequences. *No* consequences should be meted out for divergent or even antagonistic thought; such refutations should, in fact, be given additional consideration as indications of independence and bravery.
3. Tolerate all kinds of controversy, contention, and conflict, provided that no attacks are made on personalities or character, and that civil order is maintained.

    If disruption occurs, the discussion might be halted and the class alerted to the source; attention can be given to the idea of and the need for tolerance. Similarly, a distinction might be made between criticism of an act or attitude, which is permissible, and personal criticism of its holder, which is not.
4. Refrain from direct criticism of an individual or an idea—i.e., "You are wrong," or "This is wrong." It is more helpful for the teacher to ask a student to expand or explain the idea, to point out the contradictions in an argument, to suggest an opposite point of view, or to throw the idea open for general discussion than it is to tell a student that her/his contribution lacks validity.
5. Encourage students, as much as possible, to use "I" statements: "I think," "I believe," "in my opinion," etc. In this way, it is harder for the students to be elusive or evasive.

    On the other hand, it soon becomes clear if a student *needs* the cover of abstraction or impersonality ("some say," "everybody thinks," or statements in the passive voice) and should not be further pressed.
6. Build up a sense of tolerance for ideas with which he or she clearly disagrees. It is usually necessary to see some virtue in "unpleasant" thoughts, if only to understand them. Tolerance, incidentally, should not inhibit one's ability to advocate a desired course, provided that the latter is put forth reasonably as a choice to be adopted on its virtues.
7. Convey the idea that, although alternatives are equally available, they are not equally valid; *everything* is not relative.

    There *are* such things as ethical norms and standards—that is what these discussions are about—and the task of the students, individually and collectively, is to look for criteria by which a preferred set can be sought and established. Such an enterprise is tentative—and will remain so throughout a student's lifetime—but it is still worth undertaking.

8. Be prepared to handle any dissension—from the class, the administration, the community, or whatever source—that results from introducing unpopular and controversial ideas and topics. A teacher who particularly dislikes dealing with such feedback should acknowledge this and structure the class accordingly.

Very often, anticipated difficulties do not materialize; in fact, one's willingness to take risks—with material and in front of students—might equally be appreciated and applauded. In any case, honesty is usually valued, particularly by teenagers.

Teachers should not pretend that they are working in a value-free environment. Certain personal norms—achievement, ambition, effort, self-discipline, punctuality, emotional restraint—are integrated into the formal educational process, while other social values—patriotism, respect for democratic constitutional procedures, admiration of entrepreneurship, materialism—are embedded in the dominant culture. The teacher's task is not to have students reject their, or their community's preferred ideas and life-styles (although they should be free to do this, if they wish), but rather to examine and understand them. Any belief is more willingly embraced and more strongly held if backed by "good reasons"—i.e., those the belief-holder accepts as valid.

There are also the norms and standards adopted by professional groups (lawyers, doctors, businesspersons) by which their practitioners can be measured. These, too, are fitting topics for a high school social studies classroom. At one time or another, all students will be consumers of these goods and services, and some will be preparing for these kinds of careers. The ethics of the school and classroom should also not be taboo. Teenagers might be able to make more productive use of their years in secondary school if students and teachers could grasp each other's needs, goals, and constraints.

Finally, there are the ideals, goals, and values of the United States as a country and in relation to other nations—as they are expressed in national and international politics. This material is often covered in courses on government or civics or in units and time set aside for discussion of current events. Teenage students should be expected to keep themselves informed as to what is currently going on in the world, perhaps by reading a daily newspaper. But whether students are knowledgeable in this area or not, current events often generate questions on which feelings may run deep. As with other issues, the best ballast against irrationality is data. Such data might be made available for examination, particularly on issues of greater ethical import—e.g., nuclear weapons, wars, environmental impact, hunger, poverty, famine, and racism. Second, students might be warned that any extreme—over- or undervaluation, overly simplified analysis—is intellectually risky. Third, they can be told that, like it or not, such problems are *there* and are also their concern, at least to the extent that they should *think* about them.

How can the teacher guide discussions and/or work on ethical issues of all types? He or she can—

- Discuss the norms themselves as a guide to conduct in selected circumstances. Who holds these values? What is their usefulness? What do they mean, ideally and in practice? Can one live by them? Should one? What are the consequences of *not* doing so? Of doing so? Why have they been valued and observed (or valued and not observed)? Do difficulties arise in taking them seriously?

- Use the norms in problem-solving exercises. These might be third-person situations in order to sidestep the question of a personal commitment. Which values come into play in a given instance? Which choices are available to the character/actors, and what ethical/normative consequences are attached to each? Are there conflicts and trade-offs? If the student were to be the actor, what would she/he choose to do?

- Invite students to *be* the characters; ask what they would personally do in a given set of circumstances; make the same inquiry as above, but press for a greater sense of personal identification and explanation; ask them to estimate their propensities and abilities to actually carry out the standards they set.

- Ask the members of the class to list and then explore their *own* values, norms, life-styles, and preferences in terms of content, depth, and priorities. To which situations do they apply? What conflicts or consequences might be anticipated? Is there any difference between what they claim to be feeling and actual behavior? How do they feel when practice falls short of the ideal?

- Have students write up contracts specifying or requiring ethical/normative behavior codes. These codes can relate to themselves as persons or in particular roles (consumer, friend, student, family member, citizen, worker, etc.). Over a period of time, the students should report honestly and openly on performance, conflicts, consequences, contradictions, etc. Finally, they should revise the code, if necessary, to make it tighter or more livable.

Whenever possible, ethical choices should be viewed as guides to *action* in the students' environment. While the teacher cannot demand that particular steps be taken to solve or to work toward the solution to a perceived problem, she or he can be sympathetic to student action. Similarly, the class can take collective action if, by a majority vote, it decides to do so (with the minority abstaining). However, no student should be compelled to express an interest or a feeling that is not personally felt. (Noncommitment or disinterest, therefore, becomes an acceptable stance.)

If students can develop a personally chosen, internalized moral code and become aware of the ethical dimensions of all social activity, they will be able to turn their desire for achievement in useful directions. Students' acceptance and exercise of responsibility is a key concept during the high school years: responsibility for themselves; for their feelings, statements, and actions; and for their work, relationships, and community. Students should learn to be alert, inquisitive, sensitive, and reflective people. The teacher, the curriculum, and the school cannot instill these qualities in students; however, they can facilitate their emergence by providing opportunities, encouragement, and space for such development.

CONCLUSION

Thinking is a very natural act. What is unnatural is its scarcity. Critical or creative thinking is simply thinking of a higher order, by persons informed by fact and logic, insight and empathy. Critical thinking is a necessary means to problem solving, invention, and achievement. Yet it needs no justification or end: impelled by curiosity, it brings strength and satisfaction in itself.

Not every child will be taught to be a thinker, but each has the ability to become one. Children need only to continue to use the thinking process to gain awareness and command of it.

For all ages and grades, the school is a major testing ground, a place for mental experiment that can be appropriately structured and made psychologically safe. It cannot change the home or shut out the world; but it can be a bridge between and a part of both. As the focal institution of children's lives between the ages of five and eighteen, the school can help children know themselves and experience their own potentials.

Of course, the school has other, more mundane purposes as well. It teaches students specific facts and concrete skills, prepares them for a profession, and socializes them into the society in which they will most likely live as adults. Yet, none of these is antithetical to the development of the ability to think.

Many educators approach thinking as a methodology. In fact, it is not a technique, but an *act*. As with every act, performance improves by doing. It is less important that students think correctly than that they want and try to think.

The curriculum and the teacher can help facilitate students' thinking in a number of ways:

1. The teacher can set up projects that require students' thoughtful planning and execution.
2. The teacher can offer encouragement when children try to exercise their mental powers. Results should not be cast in terms of success or failure. It is better to arrive late than not to set off at all.
3. Students can be given constructive feedback—from the teacher, from classmates, and, ultimately, as they develop critical think-

ing skills, from themselves. The classroom should be an arena in which students are active and dialogue takes place.

4. An emphasis might be placed on *reaching*, rather than on attainment. Downplaying quantitative results does not mean neglecting standards. (In all situations there are minimum standards that must be met if business is to proceed.) True high standards are those ethical/normative principles that the student understands, chooses, internalizes—and keeps.

5. A key word should be *cooperation*: how each participant can be of help to the others. The student's main competitor should be him- or herself.

In the end, the school will reflect the society that maintains it. Yet the quality of that society is, in part, dependent on what happens in the school.

Thousands of years ago, the Greek philosopher Socrates said that an unexamined life is not worth living. In essence, that is what an educational process should convey. Thought—and particularly critical and creative thought—should be given high priority because it represents a human need.

BIBLIOGRAPHY

1. Ashton-Warner, Sylvia. *Teacher*. New York: Simon & Schuster, 1963.
2. Beyer, Barry K. "Improving Thinking Skills—Practical Approaches." *Phi Delta Kappan* (April 1984): 556-60.
3. Brown, Jerry L. "On Teaching Thinking Skills in the Elementary and Middle Schools." *Phi Delta Kappan* (June 1983): 709-16.
4. Bruner, Jerome S. *The Relevance of Education*. New York: W. W. Norton, 1973.
5. Coles, Robert. *The Political Life of Children*. Boston: Atlantic Monthly Press, 1986.
6. _____. *The Moral Life of Children*. Boston: Atlantic Monthly Press, 1986.
7. Cortes, Carlos E., and Richardson, Elinor. "Why in the World: Using Television to Develop Critical Thinking Skills." *Phi Delta Kappan* (June 1983): 715-16.
8. deBono, Edward. "The Direct Teaching of Thinking as a Skill." *Phi Delta Kappan* (June 1983): 706-708.
9. Dimnet, Ernest. *The Art of Thinking*. New York: Fawcett New World Library, 1966.
10. Fromm, Erich. *For the Love of Life*. New York: Free Press, 1986.
11. Glasser, William. *Schools Without Failure*. New York: Harper & Row, 1969.
12. Goodman, Paul. *Compulsory Mis-education and the Community of Scholars*. New York: Vintage, 1962.
13. Gross, Beatrice, and Gross, Ronald. *The Great School Debate*. New York: Simon & Schuster, 1985.
14. Heiman, Marcia. "Learning to Learn." *Educational Leadership* (September 1985): 20-24.
15. _____, and Slomianko, Joshua. *Critical Thinking Skills*. Washington, D.C.: National Education Association, 1985.
16. Holt, John. *Instead of Education: Ways to Help People Do Things Better*. New York: Dutton, 1976.
17. *Los Angeles Times*. "A Clash of Attention over Project Self-Esteem in Schools." November 11, 1985.
18. Michaelis, John U. *Social Studies for Children in a Democracy: Recent Trends and Developments*. Englewood Cliffs, N.J.: Prentice-Hall, 1984.
19. National Commission on Excellence in Education. In *The Great School Debate*, edited by Beatrice Gross and Ronald Gross. New York: Simon & Schuster, 1985.
20. Pascal, Blaise. *Pensées*, no. 347. 1670.

21. Postman, Neil. *Teaching as a Conserving Activity*. New York: Delacorte Press, 1979.
22. _____, and Weingartner, Charles. *Teaching as a Subversive Activity*. New York: Delacorte Press, 1969.
23. Rokeach, Milton. *The Open and Closed Mind: Investigations into the Nature of Belief Systems and Personality Systems*. New York: Basic Books, 1960.
24. Sadler, William A., and Whimbey, Arthur. "A Wholistic Approach to Improving Learning Skills." *Phi Delta Kappan* (November 1985): 199–203.
25. Shaftel, Fannie, and Shaftel, George. *Role Playing for Social Values: Decision-Making in the Social Studies*. Englewood Cliffs, N.J.: Prentice-Hall, 1967.
26. Sternberg, Robert J. "Teaching Critical Thinking, Part I: Are We Making Critical Mistakes?" *Phi Delta Kappan* (November 1985): 194–98.
27. _____. "Teaching Critical Thinking, Part II: Possible Solutions." *Phi Delta Kappan* (December 1985): 277–89.
28. White, Alan R. *The Philosophy of Mind*. New York: Random House, 1967.